Hammer of God
Aria Ligi

©2018 Aria Ligi

book design and layout: Mighty Muse, San Francisco, CA and
   SpiNDec, Port Saint Lucie, FL
cover image: *The Execution of Lady Jane Grey*, by Paul
   Delarouche, oil on canvas, 1833; The National Gallery, London

All rights reserved.

No part of this book may be used or reproduced in any manner whatsoever without written permission except in the case of brief quotations embodied in critical articles and reviews. Members of educational institutions and organizations wishing to photocopy any of the work for classroom use, or authors, artists and publishers who would like to obtain permission for any material in the work, should contact the publisher.

Printed in the United States of America.

Published by Poetic Justice Books
Port Saint Lucie, Florida
www.poeticjusticebooks.com

ISBN: 978-0-9967306-3-1

FIRST EDITION
10 9 8 7 6 5 4 3 2 1

Hammer of God
Aria Ligi

Table of Contents

Hammer of God
- Blackened at Birth   3
- Hammer of God   4
- Absolution Stain   5
- Calloused Cloven   6
- Charlotte Dreaming   7
- Unmetered Ode   8
- Tumbling Tome   9
- Tribal Tear   10

Father Destroyer
- Delivery Seal   13
- Flight of Expiation   14
- Father Destroyer   15
- Stigmata Piñata   16
- Ordination Right   17
- The Score   18

Prime Mother
- Cookie Dough   21
- Fetal Phone   22
- Prime Mother   23
- Would Chamber   25
- Salutation   26
- Heir to Bear   27
- Bunting Beam   28

Simple Blind
- Divided Stain   31
- Scalding Rome   32

Ballet in Poesy

Ballet in Poesy	35
Tone Deaf Bard	36
Casting Cabal	37
Carillon Call	38
Faery Fluting	39
Four-Flushed God	40
Exiled Unity	41
Missive Mourn	42

Vesper Bell

Borgia Betrothed	45
Shunt the Blade	46
Schism	47
La Conversazione (In three cantos, starting with Lucrezia Borgia and alternating between Lucrezia and her brother Cesare)	48
Vesper Bell	51
Confessional Ocean	52
Disrobed Snake	53
Biduous Being	54
Pseudonymous Stockholm Syndrome	55 56

Merrie Mount

Merrie Mount	59
Laudanum Sea	60
Clover Comb	61
Alveolus Brew	62
Poet Pen	63
Liar Lyre	64
Corn Queen	65

Illustrations

page 1 Hammer of God, *The Execution of Lady Jane Grey*, Paul Delarouche, oil on canvas, 1833; National Gallery, London

page 11 Father Destroyer, *The Virgin with Chancellor Rolin Luber*, detail, Jan Van Eyck, circa 1435, oil on canvas; Louvre, Paris

page 19 Prime Mother, *The Princess Diana Rose lli*, David Patterson; Fine Art America

page 29 Simple Blind, *Trey*, lithograph, Andre Largie

page 33 Ballet in Poesy, *Pointe*, Edwin A. Davis, date unknown

page 43 Vesper Bell, *Lucrezia Borgia*, Bernardino di Betto, detto Pinturicchio, 1492-1494

page 57 Merrie Mount, *La Belle Dame sans Merci*, Frank Cadogan Cowper, 1926

For Ayassa
December 21st, 1997-October 29th, 2013

Hammer of God

Blackened at Birth

My existence was a mistake,
Pondered on in the empty hours
And under fingers that clutch the grave.

My existence puzzled the purity of faith.
Devil, blasphemer penance which fell on pageantry
Spike kneed vestments and eyes agape.

My existence came with a price,
Paid, and paid, and paid
The push here swift and clean.

A falling, tumbling splintering, divvying
Pitted and racked- gutting
But leaving me no less fooled.

A bloodied banded orb
Dressing the unopened packaging.

Hammer of God

Why don't you let the hammer of god rain down on me;
The gibbet tied tightly in your bloodied fists~
Why don't you take the mallet so, heavy;
Made from the old hickory that stood behind our privy,
And hack and hack till my brains smack.
No more to torment you.
No more to sully the purity of your low hanging vine,
Of your sweet Christ wine-
Of your hymnals sitting as brethren on the pews sublime.

To think is absolute freedom-
To question, is to shine.
These things professed as unmitigated truth,
Now rot and twist are stamped divine~

The call of so many voices pursued me,
Out of the darkness you consumed me.
I ran till my breath nearly broke,
And your god became, what he was, unmasked.
His teeth shown bared emitting bracken flares,
Within the vacuum of his oracular tomb.
His hammer is his tongue, his teeth are the blade,
Serrated edge ripping me to shreds.

In the blaspheme, in the sour bilious breeze,
The hammer sounds, the tree is felled -I am free.

Absolution Stain

Good morning America, do you hear my cry;
The unborn epiphanies never to arise.
This mouth nakedly open could swallow you-
Who lie blinded and wounded by your own hand,
Filtering for coins in the burnt and mildewed lands.

Good morning to the fields of chaff, ears broken,
Wrinkled and weeds untilled, the plough sits corroded,
Fettered by ill use. Eyes peer out amidst the blades
Hurling and railing insults on the bloodied shafts
Once stained, in the green rich mulch and morning dew.

Good morning to what, a goodness now tainted in suspicion,
The milk soured by invectives and soil riddled in derision.
This pen that inks the page, stands unapologetic in the rain.

Calloused Cloven

Slip a finger thru the quire so unobtrusive
Do I aspire.

Do I dare beyond this ~To muse past hope;
Brave~ a gallant page.

My fingers muff sliced by bars
Transparent yet gilded in sacrilege.

I hear the screams o'er blue bottomed hills
Hovering o'er mines.
They wave hatchets thru the pages and blistering roads.

My fingers lift- chapped and bowed yet, not broken- not torn,
The splinter shifts and dies under the peeling spine.

Charlotte Dreaming

I was born into this ether or either,
And the smoke funneling sifting fumes.
Cattails swaying between my mother's knees and womb.
I was assailed: demon lover of the blood ringed moon.

I was a curse unnamed on their name, on being,
Of what was expected.
And he nearly cast me into the night swamped sea.
He would have drowned me.
A candy wrapper tossed down as debris.

The label held stuck to me, inwardly is where I dwelt,
Gainst tribe and the wound.
Branded ~ a searing badge summoning me away,
Where no voices could hear, no chorus of peers.
No angels choir to dance or sing for me.

I became my own chorale.
Wreathed myself with florid laurels,
Of lilies and violets and roses too.
No one brought them for me, no hosannas peeled the air,
But I await the light, and it will find me there.

Unmetered Ode

Little worm unspooling from the pink pooled prism,
Oozing intemperate working, webbing, pitiless threatening.

Extraction is no matter, like a hydra, it re-tools again.
Sick Dali wannabe, whipping out and firing its parasitic skein.

Take me in so I remember, how to dismember,
This self-inflicted life.

Tumbling Tome

In the hopes that you hear this let us go
Where exiguous missives are deemed sacred truth.

The child's knees perforate, clanking bells warbling
A dissonant dirge tossing her on that solemn journey,
To that hot oiled, boiling bubbling road.

Oh, gauged road blistering the soul.
Let her stand, bold till the road hardens- cold,
Melting and slithering in the rage worn day.

Tribal Tear

Seeing out from within, crudely woven, tightly bound
Brackets bracing me, animal in my house of embryonic sin,
Buttressed at birth, a dungeon to kin.

They want my blood upon the brazier.
How the glistening tinder flies into the night air.

To cleave gainst this, the path would dim.
My feet falter hooded, shaking, quaking, clan forsaking,
Risking all for the open air.

Father Destroyer

Delivery Seal

I felt nothing when you died, crawling out of the veil of lies
Was an onerous task setting aside the ranting, booming,
caterwauling of you, in your final glory prophesying my ruin.

To touch me someone had to be sick in the head.
That is what you said.
I felt nothing when you died, that of course is the biggest lie.
A shudder swept through me-relief and emptiness.

It is an oddity that your boundless apostrophizing
Can still echo within me more heavily than the hands
Tightening about my ankles face pumping vermillion,
Veins pushing through skin.

You hung me upside down -swinging effigy, waiting
For the hands to ride my ass in that resounding, dystopic
Rhythm wailing, railing, teeth grinding, my head spinning
In an ethereal out of body sway, strangely comatose
With a strident grandeur.

From that upside down, turned around point of view
I could see the smile creeping through.
Your paternal greatness was bound to the stage,
Of how and who and what people would say.
Yet, this queerness lingered and flung about me- like a noose,
Unseen, unscarred, emotional remains.

I did not cry when you died, I had no tears to shed.
Out of the coffin insulated bed I fled,
Yet time would spin me back to you- and to that place-
Hushed in whispers shrouded in screams-

Where to be, a woman was to be prey,
To voice dissent was only a dream.

Flight of Expiation

Aside this genteel decree
We pulled the tides gainst pride and efficacy.

Are the lies which cling to robes dripping in blood portend
Any different than the vagrant
Hiding behind the confessional divulging his sins.

Is he cast out or laid bare;
While like Christ thru our tears,
We cleanse his feet in showers,
Waiting for the reign of absolution.

Father Destroyer

His pear worn face boring and impugning,
Renouncing and lying,
Hands that could bestow mercy or flail in the name of Christ.

Oh, Pontiff pure. Father destroyer,
Your scepter is jagged wheeled and impure.
You lay siege, Your, eyes bleed.

Swimming gondoliers thru the wreckage you have secured.
Thy head is bent in apostolic reverence.
The thistles that crown you do not immure

Whilst I, in my blackened being,
Heave and sigh for understanding,
Into the darkened hoard.

Stigmata Piñata

Your big boot, iron heeled maw,
Stamps down on the clamor of Italy.

Oh humanity!
The weighted root sticks, poison hoofed sleuth.

Into my tongue, into my womb, tired insidious viper.
There, there is no wielding.
There- there is no feeling.

While the axe finds its way to the nape,
And severs all it saw.

Ordination Right

Ho low, he crept down ferreting the earthen hollow.
Skulking usurper, teething seraph's entrails-
He supped and supped from the red river's cup,
Till the puckered sac set agape and the germ was laid.
Perpetual stain, rounding the sallow opening,
To the tunnel once pristine,
Where he left, the wastrel chained.

The Score

Now that you are dead I hear you no more;
The conversation lies unfinished.
Glyphs fragmentary trills, lilting soprano dubious and shrill.

Sheets soaked and rife in rancor bleed no more
For the duet, we played has stilled.
Voices, hushed and subsumed by your steel-toned will,
The composition incomplete settles in being.

Restraining the notes, pitched canticles,
Pinging and piping gainst arch puncturing the meat
Which spills a putrid dystopic lingering smell.

I hear you no more; I am deafened in cottoned bound chords
The conductor lays down his baton,
And walks within the endless score.

Prime Mother

Cookie Dough

I don't plan to eat flour or pretend it is, what it is not
A cookie, cake or croissant
I won't cry for a particle, an eighth of a spoon,
A dash of salt spilt like a lithe snowflake.

These things sit apart, unmixed, unbaked.
The chemical process not yet begun.
To do so, would be a sham mock play,
Solely acclaimed for visions and dreams.
The, what could have been, cut like the edgings sniped seams.

Does the baker stand before his stores and dream of pastries;
Smooth shiny silk frosting, multicolored hues,
Before even an egg has been gored.
That was more than this. At this moment
That egg, was a perfect chick.

Yet, who mourns the loss of that flawless yellowed being.
We cast it in -just another ingredient in the bowl-
The egg was already a formed being,
Waiting to be self-or drowned in the soupy bin.

Yet, we stand above,
At the larder of life and judge what is, as less than.
We lament the loss.
We ache and berate ourselves-over what.

If we could set aside the moral posturing,
And the political, emotional ranting,
And see each distinct- discrete part -Yet, not the whole,
We find, we do not have even the base,
For that delicious cookie dough.

Fetal Phone

The eyes that peer out, they do not see,
Fingers that tussle, flailing fervently neath shadows' light
All- encompassing home where feeling is as yet inured,
And time moves on sleepy trundled legs.

When I awake to the moaning & shrieking
Will you carry me, self- assured tucked at the hip
In the crevice combing, which in its roundness reflects
The familiar of what had been home;

Will you reach within and find me;
Imperfect as I am:
Someone, or will you take and take,
& knowing the cost drive in the stake.

To my being, innocent, inclusion marring the mirage & fact
Abort me, I scream; cut the crimped & wrinkled thread.
Did I write that, yes, the threat to your freedom, & time;
That could be better spent.

Abort me, so the seed does not take form,
Rip me from your vestal arms,
So, I'll not stain the aching need.
Purge this pestilence from your self-important being.

This is harder than the ravages of bulimia, fingers shoved
Down the esophagus in a mighty expunging of self-hate.
With this you can honor your soul, leave me out of it,
Pretend I never was.

Abort me now, to live knowing you are unwanted,
& worse, that you never were, sinks within the skin,
Hidden unbidden, while the knife disappears
& your being dims.

Prime Mother *

Oh, prime mother, are you blind to the dross, godly entail,
Bequeathed to your progeny.
The subtle subtext lacing that foaming effervescent sea.

This bequest was yours alone to give.
It was seen in the faces & hearts.
In the flowers that lined & made your final bed.

Would you recognize him, the smile situated plainly;
Under guile and toothy gums when pageantry is gone,
& the lights dim.
Will he still be your sweet gentle ingenuous child.

Oh, prime mother, does he dream of you still,
& does that image wax & press within it
The promise susurrated, the unaffected life.

The image, you censured.
Does he hear you anymore;
Does he acknowledge the implications;

Oh, prime mother, your smile still shines in his eyes.
Let your open arms adorn him.
Let the humble pathos be conceded.

No more to be suborned in convenient conventionality.
Upset the sett- tear the style from your bosom.
Oh, Primal mother, hear our plea.

The monarchial choir, where Bobbies nod refrains
A hideous discordant act of duty.
Throw the cockade to the sea.
Channel a ballooning polluted pledge to aristocracy.

Turn your air brushed cheek, rosette powdered & keen
To the last; hinting, abiding for that silent kiss.
Would we be remiss to stand on, awaiting, for;
Her slight form to hail us from beyond.

Oh, Prime mother, your anthem has been acceded
To the halls of the aged and the poor, whose little limbs
Frail as tinder, lovely embers lit the hillocks.

Crackling & spinning, dwindling & dying.
Furious lights descending the hearse's motor now diminishing
The flame she lit as none before.

* For Princess Diana of Wales

Would Chamber

Would that she would bear it, under the blarney breech,
And in the surf- pain swear it was greater than
Not lesser than the seed.

Could she hold it in; could she tear it from its bunker;
Where the nestled heart- beat,
Half formed, half torn palpitating with discordant measure,

Would this nearness to her own; constant inside
The queenly throne, keep it safe from the terror,
Coffin lacquered and blackened bones.

Shadows now enthrall & leave us wondering in vacant halls,
Where choice is a distant call, we make in whispers,
Wishing for answers from that silent chamber.

Salutation

I can think about this now without shuddering.
Voices echo trailing and fluttering behind a wake.
Oh, requiem of the interred on pink grey granite refined.

My fingers walk on yellowed keys, blackened by the aged
And fallowed ease.

I can see your face, hear the quiver,
While lips, pruned & pasted coral, ache to voice, the unseen,

And dance the darkened dream; sons who never were
Standing in crisp white and blue,
Salute her as a soldier would quiet, intrepid and absolute.

Heir to Bear *

What do they matter those tiny feet, twigs;
Lissome stilts and sweet as figs.

What is the cost to our humanity.
To our self-proclaimed united, nobility.

We abate-We capitulate gainst primogeniture,
Titled heirs and the pomposity
Which somehow lifts us, silent and unawares.

Under their spell, we walk dream bound,
For that promised pinnacle.

We wander through candy fumed clouded rooms
Where the opiates, orgiastic take us in,
Wreathing us in its portentous doom.

The cacophony of the unheralded is a hammer on my tongue
Which coughs & rasps, a little purr stamped as frippery.

And breathing (now an arduous task) subdues the slight sac,
In its naked, nascence which, was never brilliant, nor fulsome.

But lays its soft head between her shaking knees, inert,
While the leavings, viscous sheen dried & the announcement
of the day, of the imminent arrival died, unpronounced.

No dais to adorn him, no mantle decked in purple pageantry
Proclaimed his majesty.

But gainst his mother's slicked and sweat raked cheeks
He found dignity.

---

* On the birth of Prince William's son; for the 700 babies born into poverty each day in Britain.

Bunting Beam *

Little being loin-and lion seated,
Take your scepter and orb,
Splay it outward, beguiling latticed flower,
Fomenting furiously, harvesting dearly
The bread needed as never before.

*For Prince George of Cambridge, born 7/22/13

Simple Blind

Divided Stain*

It is not with a blade tipped-nor abased,
This masquerade of black boy's bodies on parade.

Do their corpses float, unbent-unbroken
Above our field of plane.
Whispering raining, softly the silent shrieks,
Then no more the pain.

*For Trayvon Martin 7/14/13

Scalding Rome

By a country marketing machismo-mores deemed norm.
Railing tribalistic chants, feudalistic, futile and forlorn.
I have no sympathy for this pock marked crater riddled
Fracture tongued idiocy.

With its supposed suppositions, hateful proclamations,
Where Ministers can inflame statements insane,
Gainst a culture alien as Orangutans,
For the minor tone, a pigment deepening in their cranium.

Words and attitudes loathsome and inane,
There is no peal to this refrain,
Because reason is a prisoner choking on its own chain.
Up for air, up for air where none remains.

And ears once innocent now bow inward,
Gainst the weight of that rusty harangue.

Ballet in Poesy

Ballet in Poesy

To work in constant fluidity amassing equanimity.
How can we place our toes upon the keys;
Or pirouette poetically.

Each foot embracing the line on heel and pointe,
Arching out, aching upward,
In movement and in flight.

Tone Deaf Bard

I am weary of idiosyncratic syllables.
Roses sewn in dung dipped barbs.

Slippery slough filled; the phlegmatic hindrance
Beats its mighty fists upon rocks,
Shoulders, boulders of the Bards.

Shouting-railing, that their lyres sing verse,
When all I hear is a tone-deaf chord.

Casting Cabal

I saw his cradled head under the wounded flowerbed,
Wrinkled and sagging in its frowzy spinal fare.
It didst spake, unbeknownst to maternal ears:
See me, hear me, climb unrestrained from your womb.

But their eyes were waxened o'er.
Soused in the nectar of faery flower.
Whilst ears and hands mourned the loss,
They had as yet to partake.

They in that mournful hour, wailing their loss,
Lauded the passing not so much as an abysmal parting;
But with acquiescence turned their knowing gaze,
Whispered sad and ironic clichés – contrition
For the woe, bludgeoned muse-

That they were now sacred in their loss,
Gilded in ethereal dross.
Lofty gold hues which are embossed.
To the saddened and the few- the exclusive conclave.
The drearisome and entitled brave.
Touted martyrs and saints while the doors slam.

And the tissues are packed away.
We are left, bemused and despised.
Our entreaties of compassion sit in tatters.
And his lone voice remains unheard.
In its opulent defiant refrain: "see me", "hear me"
As the dirt pours on his open grave.

Carillon Call

Could I have lost my soul in you.
Not in a soul bonded bounded sensual colonnade.
In the cloister of sisterhood, that convent divine.
I turn away my throat, constricting, opining.
How sad to think my feet- Unsaddled, toes;
Thru habit and time, riddled on the puzzle, intricate- delicate.

I am too old for conjugating,
Or to memorize their Latin prayers.
My priory is for me alone,
Not to hide as one sequestered,
Nimbly climbing the beaded poesy.

These stone walls know me well,
I return untouched to this familiar citadel.
Unafraid yet, not brave,
Unmoored, recompense paid,
My feet will find the way.

Faery Fluting

Olona, Oh Olona the faery being
Sat upon the tip just petering.

O'er the blade swift and slippery sheath,
Cool and wax slicked under her knobby knees.

Olona, Oh Olona, thy wings beat,
A pulsating palpitating rhythm,
That slights and quenches my being.

Is the draught of nectar sweet;
For the bees find it an erotic feast.
Is it finer than claret and richer than cabriolet;

Olona, Oh Olona pluck the chords from my throat,
While you play Apollo's, lyre note by note.

Four-Flushed God

Oh, the pomposity of that piping paternal pen.
You low, cleaving, skulking unctuous men!
You twist and imbibe cruel invectives cast as knives,
Skewering and felling each syllable
Whilst wreathing your quill with chaplets.

Dais's bejeweled velveteen tools,
Stealing yea infecting honorariums to Apollo.
Whose hallowed halls stand desecrated and deflowered.
Sacred chalices of sages and scribes.
Their gleam now seen as tarnished leavings,
Yet still cast within each sun hewn ray,
The felting and hammered gold of yesterday.

Exiled Unity

The loss, eternal, wiles away.
Blindly burrowing searing and scoring into abasement.

The return of this nomad.
This intrepid soldier of the pit.
To its secret secreted displaced self.

Where she once hid,
Was her flight a willing sojourn,
Once more on her knees.

The martyr,
Still longing for, still searching for that unknown dignity.

Missive Mourn

The pen inverts upon me piercing the sternum.
This is where you sat.
This is where nesting, small eaglet cooing,
Amongst white fluffed feathers,
That bent and swirled my girth, mother to her egg.

Now a marbled, glaucous, softened mass,
And the pen- prodigious quill,
Bleeds no more on the porous page,
Beckoning you against your will.

Vesper Bell

Borgia Betrothed *

If I could have lain within your finery
Would you have taken me;
Your lance broken, as merely a token,
Downing a dead tree.

Would you have taken me, as a queen;
Emancipated from mores,
Where to flaunt within familial bonds,
Pledging- dousing in the ichor of debauchery.

Unleashed tongues grappling gnashing,
Hooks amongst seams weaving indelicacies.
Would you take me; Knightly, not as brother;
But as friend and lover.

Your knees a quake, your hands forsake,
All the parchment, All the laws forbidding.
We would break the stave,
Living depraved, equal and no more slaves.

*For Lucrezia Borgia to her brother Cesare

Shunt the Blade

The searing jagged jabs to the hole, will not make you whole.
Nor atone for the quiet death, that burning branded as a hot
Smoldering, unfaltering note, over and over the bludgeoning
Pain till it tore up my thighs and left me insane.
I put my head upon the splice begging you for my life.

While under the wretched bovine knife you hacked &
hacked.
Slung me in your gunny sack, bones chiseled shards en mass;
Over the blood hewn ice. The ringing in my ears reverberated
Through ribs and tears, till fear and anger overwhelmed me.
I lay in an ocean replete where none could reach, nor hear.
Tired child of doom let your sadness not o'er take you nor
Hatred, make you; let it still be immaculate seed.

Schism

It is safe now, to speak the name.
To say it.
To acknowledge; disclosure reveals, but does not blame.
It is safe now, the shadows,
Phantoms whose befouled cone left me, sunken & enclosed,
While the walls took me in.

It is safe now to no longer need.
Or hear reflected back my own nihilistic epiphanies.
His hands, his lips which clouded & passed judgement,
While the breath slid in.
It is safe now to dream,
Because there is more than him.

La Conversazione (In three cantos, starting with Lucrezia Borgia and alternating between Lucrezia and her brother Cesare)

I.

Where have you been, brother friend.
Never far, never near.
Just beyond fingers that would hold you,
Into me-in me, constant, though unsettling.

I am aware of this distance, it can ne'er be breached.
The waters which divide us stand, house upon the sand,
Glinting, golden cockles about your brow,
Floating wavelet your man-child eyes see me-but do not.

The ache cinches constricting and clawing
Robbing me, raping me, while I stand here bloodied
And the blood, our blood flows like a river
Down the blade.

We don't think these things, the thoughts themselves
Verboten. Could you have ever said them in my presence
Your hands tremble eyes, London blue, cool as the ocean,
Slip through.

Brimming tears, you dare not shed,
Dread laden -dead.
While my hands and lips would wait forever
For the remittance that never will be.

This would be our final hour.
This would be our last hoorah.
This would be our solo foray into the wave,
Where words are not tainted and love is not stained.

Let us come up from the sea.
In the light of day; let us be brave.

II.

Not brave, no knight stands before you.
Only the mirage -twisted, fright filled knave.
To see you is not simply torture.
It is my crucifixion.

The curls upon my brow convolve,
Bristles jimmying into the emulsified core,
Where memory waits.
My hands upon you,

Hands that would clasp
And then compound as cement
Into that sweet honeyed nave,
Into your crystal prism intemerate cave.

Or the foot and heel- steel,
Wailing against brittle molded bone,
Crushing the central point- tiny tinder twigs,
Pubic symphysis against your vulva-velvet dome.

Did I do this;
Club, club to rub out what was.
Did I do that thing so hateful to you,
The one most loved.

Or was it desire;
Feeding and nesting on fire,
While with a pitchfork, the stabs came inwardly
Secretly so, though forever without sin.

I close my mouth against the words, lest they escape –
Prisoners on the run.
We scream sanctuary, not from them,
But from the voices huddled within.

III.

In my dreams, it was gentler.
There were no bouts, fists and feet,
Heel as staves raging in paroxysms
While the room dropped, and spun.

In the quietude,
Between night and dawn we lay
The thrum of your beating, thundering warmth
Heart inside my skin.

There you would ne'er voice it.
Nor wink in self-assured acclamation.
Within your breast, certainty beamed,
And the blade was sheathed.

I could hear you low, unafraid,
Though the reckless and galling sea
Pitched and tossed me o'er the railing, heart submerging
Neath the cool black glass tempered pane.

Away, away from the surety of your gaze.
The unsteady rage.
In my dreams, it was a gentler thing,
And the words themselves remembered.

Not the sour lit craze,
But the solid glowing flame.
Not the fists shooting death drones
Into the secret place where Venus reigns.

Not the dusky hours of screams unanswered.
My innocence deflowered, but the canon writ of love,
Which in its beauty is silent;
But not extinguished.

Vesper Bell

We must put the flame away.
Douse the rippling embers,
Dodge the quickening blue;
Its rapid tongue yellow'd sparkling, mute, unyielding.

Where we once rolled down the stairs, King and Queen,
Our mother feared we were fornicating.
And the thought must have slip't like prayer.

In your ears -there it stayed a solid darkened ecstasy,
Sitting behind the sheer drapery, chiffon lacing
Light wafting white hiding, shadowing the deepening.
It only came out as a waif worn orphan wild.

In the cries you sang, low guttural trills
Words inferred,
But never stated.
She said we were, she feared we may.

And the words themselves, even now,
Hang within thought and air, like a prayer.

Confessional Ocean

I have dunked in the original sin.
Dipped my head under,
Not even attempting to tread water.
Attrition is bared and the bloodied beads wear.
Does the box lower under the rim of the ocean floor;
Where my head is swimming and breath is obdured.

Disrobed Snake

My words are redacted pleas,
Falling, dying in tombs of vapidity.
I am on my knees, wobbly pinions stunted, blunted
By the unanswered master of the symphony.

His words are callow incisions,
Foraging, slinking, staining infecting;
While in the sweetness of his breath venomous fumes sway,
Sucking, honing with laser like precision,
For that soft hallowed juncture-
Where jousting at the point of the blade,
Would leave me slayed- yet unafraid.

Biduous Being

Who will he be when he crosses the line;
The threshold into my being.
Will the face that I behold be the devil;
Lips cool as glass, wisps emitting sulfuric ash.

Or will he be the one who steps in me,
Arms unfolding, eyes knowing, deepening azure,
Yet cool, cool, cool.
Will his hands caress my hair or furl into granite;
Wailing and carving my nether ware.

Who will he be Lover, killer, or kindred.
Never friend.
The blood that runs in me has stained him too-
On this dam, we stand united -consecrated,
In love and fear, hate and despair.

Who will he be;
He is me.

Pseudonymous

I am baring it out completely, not in the niceties of bows,
But revealing-ne'er concealing -what it was.
While you laid me on the rock.
Whilst you lay with me draped and torn in the dark.
It was there, unabashed without delay,
This love I carried.

Not your fervent wish- not the mask.
Deist with your broken crown, the golden crest –
Familial pledge unbound, but the washed and naked being,
Glistening and stealing the sleep from my eyes.
The treasured pleasure of each sunrise.
My love for you- battered and torn,
By your hands, crimson and warm,
Remains -the wayward being- waiting to be born.

Stockholm Syndrome

I don't live in Stockholm, not that I ever did.
The diaphanous blanched flakes,
Blinding me as we coursed thru the cooling drifts.

I don't yearn for Stockholm, like I once did.
Thinking freedom reigned there.
My wanting unencumbered by truth and drudgery,
I painted only poesy.

And lifted you high above the fjords, as if on display,
Your breast plate and stolid horns, erect shafts,
Piercing the sunless day.

I haven't dreamed of Stockholm
Since you stormed from the chalet.
The door to that domicile is locked,
And the snow has blown away.

Merrie Mount

Merrie Mount

Little hillock of honey, mound of resplendence,
Let us crest the ambo and light the orb.
In raining, shower the equipage,
Complete each fairway and byway,
The road to evermore.

Laudanum Sea

Ah, the infinite ache, nesting, netting ~slithering and slinking
Under your skin ~there to take you in,
Lover, drifter, consummate pretender.
That you matter, that you are that ray of sun,
Quintessential fulcrum ~hovering where no one dares,
Into the night you will fly unawares.

Oh, shimmering sun!
Don't let the moon eclipse your brilliance.
The weight you carry is a Cat 'O nine tales,
Cutting and cruising through the boom and the slit torn sail.
We are riding the nightmare cutter on an ocean of glass,
Prism~ prison flecked and flawed,
Under the seams and into the gnashing jaws.

Clover Comb

Dulcet highland nether mound, mounted in acquiescence.
Was it easy, or did it bend as bread,
Wafer of heaven on my tongue.

Did it break, that mound,
A harmonious aspect of the holy gift unspoken.

Oh, most silent mother, protector of the crust,
Crumbs of Christ your son.

Did you raze the mound;
Folding within on that sanctified original sin.

Did it stain the shadows in that darkened den;
Or is it, as it ever was: the unsoilt hole.
Floating on the breath of brethren.

Alveolus Brew

The light shines thru the octagonal décolleté,
T's a slick shoot down the ichor riddled frappé.
Petals as balloons sail by,
While brilliants festoon, amber and golden,
Gilding each cell, feckless and unbroken.

The precious preserve slowly ambles the hidden gorge,
Where once, she, on her mightily plinth bared haunches,
Queenly and distinct, cleaved and birthed each nestled orb.
Into the bunker, into its regal store.

There to ferment and cradle the golden tincture.
Panacea to the poor.
The preponderance is miniscule and doled out in dribbles,
Between knotted knuckles crinkled papyrus.

And the prune puckered lips, which quiver,
Canals, slipping and funneling,
Venetian gondoliers on the golden river,
Waving and swimming for life.

Poet Pen

Oh, sacrificial spell!
The bard who cups the shaft and bosom,
Trills in me~ platitudes, elegies, hosannas.

Stand aft to take it in.
Yea winsome notes fie high, fie low.
Round, and round and in me~ he goes!

Liar Lyre

Flying buttresses on display.
Wiling lines of sophistic phrase.
Hackneyed ~hauteur singularly seen,
As if from Orpheus's silver strings.
Tho the lyre rings no merrie tune,
But stands a bow bent poisoned bolete,
The cap~ crusted polluted stool,
Expelling and feigning majesty,
Whilst mocking the unseen, ethereal tulle.

Corn Queen

She runs thru flaxen beams.
Lightsome limbs whirling,
Ah -so san souci.

She is the being that graces the flowers.
Quaff be-dewed ne'er dour.
Winking, gleaming in that bow-bent boat,
For the draught- sheen reigning supreme.

acknowledgments

Thank you to the editors of the following publications in which these poems appeared:

Fantasy Realm
  Faerie Fluting

Light Journal Issue Five Reflections
  Stockholm Syndrome

New Poetry 2015
  La Conversazione (In three Cantos, starting with Lucrezia Borgia and altering with her brother Cesare)

New Poetry 2016
  Hammer of God
  Prime Mother
  Heir to Bear
  Casting Cabal
  Shunt the Blade

New York's Best Emerging Poets Anthology, Z Publications
  Ordination Right

October Hill Winter Issue 2017
  Pseudonymous

Still Here, VLP Magazine, 2014, University of South Dakota
  Cookie Dough

www.ingramcontent.com/pod-product-compliance
Lightning Source LLC
Chambersburg PA
CBHW050445010526
44118CB00013B/1693